Table of Contents

Introduction

Jesus Christ the same yesterday, today, and forever Heb 13:8. Jesus is still in the business of healing through His Body as He ever was. Many are learning to exercise this part of the nature of Christ in us through training in Schools of Healing. A School of Healing can be employed to teach every member of a Church or Ministry how to operate in Healing. Healing is one of the Keys of the Kingdom that is instrumental to see its advancement and to harvest souls. As many in the Body of Christ well know this is the season that the Lord is releasing the knowledge of His Glory in the earth as the waters covers the sea. Healing and Miracles should be the norm and not the exception. Many have been praying and longing to see the Glory of God manifesting in signs and wonders. I believe this is our set time.

The Lord desires to heal in every service, meeting, street corner and in every sphere of society. Often an anointing of healing comes in during our worship services but is not discerned due to time restraints and insensitivity to the Holy Spirit. With a well administered healing ministry we can minister to the sick and bound on a consistent basis as well as used to be a tool for the salvation of the lost.

I have personally seen cancer healed, knee caps replaced (supernaturally), and the healing of arthritis just to name a few. After imparting to others, testimonies have come in of them laying hands on the sick in their own sphere of influence and seeing them recover. By God's grace through Schools of Healing many have testified publicly of their healing and being empowered to heal. This manual is designed to help you and your ministry to be equipped to flow in the healing and miracle anointing.

This is the time to equip the Body of Christ. The Lord has set in His church according to I Corinthians 12:28 the gifts of healing and miracles. Let's see them established and blessing the Church and the World. Thank you and be blessed.

If you desire a School of Healing and Miracles, or School of the Prophets and Prophetic Intercession please contact us at healing.prayer@ymail.com.

HEALING DIMENSIONS

Dimension (Latin, "measured out") is a parameter or measurement required to define the characteristics of an object— i.e. length, width, and height or size and shape.

The Lord has distinctive varieties and distributions of the Healing anointing. The areas we will primarily be covering in these lessons are: healing through Deliverance (from demonic oppression), healing through the Presence of God, healing through Laying on of Hands by Faith, healing through the Word of God, and healing through the Word of Knowledge. Because of the variety of ways the Lord has provided for us to be healed, we need not wait for just one particular administration. We can look to God for healing in a variety of ways.

We have a Covenant of Healing with the Lord that was bought for us by His love through the stripes of Jesus. Healing was purchased for us by the scourging and the Cross of Jesus Christ.

Healing is a dimension of the Love of Christ. We see in Ephesians the third chapter and the eighteenth verse that the Apostle Paul's desire was *"That you may have the power and be strong to apprehend and grasp with all the saints, (God's devoted people, the experience of that love) what is the breadth and length and height and depth (of it); amp.*

God's desire is for us to be strong and apprehend the power of His love in all its dimensions. He heals us because He loves us.

"Now there are distinctive varieties and distributions of endowments (gifts, extraordinary powers distinguishing certain Christians, due to the power of divine grace operating in their lives by the Holy Spirit) and they vary, but the Holy Spirit remains the same. And there are distinctive varieties of service and ministration, but it is the same Lord (Who is served). And there are distinctive varieties of

operation (of working to accomplish things), but it is the same God Who inspires and energizes them all in all. ..... To another the extraordinary powers of healing by the same Spirit: To another the working of miracles....
(I Cor. 12:4-6 & 9b & 10a) amp.

DISTINCTIVE VARIETIES

Here is a list of the dimensions of healing some of which we will discuss later in more details in other chapters.

- Healing through deliverance
- The healing presence
- Prayer of Faith
- Healing through the Logos Word
- Healing by word of knowledge
- Healing of the Emotions
- Healing of the broken Heart
- Physical healing
- Mental healing
- Healing from Rejection or Betrayal

Reflections

1. Name three ways by which the Lord
    will heal you.

2. Is there a medical solution for the
    spirit of infirmity?

3. What are three areas in which a
    person may need healing.

4. Why does God desire to see His
   people healed?

5. According to I Corinthians 12 what
   ways does the Holy Spirit manifest
   the gifts?

Notes

OUR COVENANT OF HEALING

Healing is part of our covenant that we have in the Lord Jesus Christ as believers. God heals believers because of covenant; He heals the unsaved because of His mercy. We will look at healing as a tool to harvest souls later. We will begin to see healing through the covenant more clearly as we take a look at these verses found in Isaiah. All references are taken from strong's exhaustive concordance.

Surely He hath borne our griefs, and carried our sorrows: yet we did esteem Him stricken, smitten of God, and afflicted. But He was wounded for our transgressions, He was bruised for our iniquities the chastisement of our peace was upon Him; and with His stripes we are healed. (Isaiah 53:4-5)

Now we will look at some of the major words that Isaiah uses in the original Hebrew language that we may get a greater understanding of what he is saying.

v. 4-**Borne** ref# 5375- pardon, carried away, wear take away utterly, received

Greif's ref# 2483- anxiety, calamity, disease, sickness
Sorrows ref# 4341- anguish, affliction, grief, pain sorrow

v.5-***Wounded*** ref# 2490- derived from 2470- to become weak, sick, be diseased, infirmity, put to pain
Transgression ref# 6588- revolt (national, moral or religious), rebellion - to break away (from just authority), trespass, quarrel, offend

Bruised refs# 1792- to crumble, beat to pieces, break in pieces, crush, destroy
Bruised- an injury to ones feeling, spirit, etc. (Emotional healing) <u>Webster New World College Dictionary</u>
Iniquity ref# 5771- fault, punishment, sin

Peace ref# 7965- (shalom), health, prosperity, peace, happiness, favor
7965 from ref# 7999- to be safe (in mind, body or estate), to be completed, finish, full, restore

Stripes ref# 2250- bruises, hurt, wound, black and blue mark
2250 from ref# 2266- to join, couple together, have fellowship with, join together

Healed ref# 7495- (raphah), to mend (by stitching), to cure, cause to heal, physician, repair thoroughly, make whole

I Cor. 11:24-25 - States that His body was broken for us and that His blood was the New Testament. The word testament is strong's ref. # 1242 and it means covenant.

What a mighty God we serve! Behold what love the Father has bestowed upon us. The cross of Christ purchased so much for us. Everything we need has been completed for us through Christ sufferings during the crucifixion.

Now, if Jesus took our grief's, infirmities, and sicknesses and bore them on the cross, then we shouldn't have to bare them as well. All the Lord needs and is looking for is someone to take Him at His word and act on it. When we believe the word of God through these verses are true we will have more faith to believe the Lord for our healing and for the healing of others. These verses are to be meditated on in the light of the broader Hebrew meaning. There's life in these verses. These verses have the power to save lives.

The Lord said in John 6:63 that,

It is the spirit that quickeneth; the flesh profiteth nothing: the words that I speak unto you, they are spirit, and they are life.

REFLECTIONS

1. What does the cross of the Lord Jesus the Christ of God mean to you?

2. Name some of the benefits that we obtained from the scourging and the cross that the Lord went through.

3. Give a scriptural example of Jesus healing someone because of the covenant?

4. Is healing only for those of the covenant? Give a scriptural example.

5. Give three scriptures explaining the mercy of God.

Notes

HEALING THROUGH DELIVERANCE

Now Jesus was teaching in one of the synagogues on the Sabbath. And there was a woman there who for eighteen years who had an infirmity caused by a spirit (a demon of sickness). She was bent completely forward and utterly unable to straighten herself up or to look upward. And when Jesus saw her, He called (her to Him) and said to her, Woman, you are released from your infirmity! Then He laid (His) hands on her, and instantly she was made straight, and she recognized and thanked and praised God. (Luke 13:10-13) amp.

During our worship services in our local churches we not only have those who need to be set free from spirits of rejection, hurt and other obvious emotional bondages, but also spirits of sickness, disease and infirmity. When a person who is dealing with a spirit of infirmity visit the doctor's office they will sometimes hear "we can't find what the problem is." Someone under the influence of the spirit of infirmity may not be responding to medication and may live a sickly life. In any case we should ask the Lord if there are curses in operation or if the spirit of infirmity is involved.

Discernment is much needed when contending for the health of an individual. You may also ask the individual if the sickness has been diagnosed in other members of the family on either side to see if it is generational and if so it may be a curse. If it is found that a curse is involved, by the Spirit of the Lord or by discerning through the reoccurrence in the family bloodline then the curse would have to be broken and the spirit cast out before the healing can occur. When dealing with demon spirits one must be sensitive because sometimes the spirit will go during the time the person is being prayed for with the commandment to be healed and at other times it must be dealt with and forced out separately. A healing minister must be sensitive to the Holy Spirit so his degree of accuracy will be higher. He must relax and listen prophetically.

If when praying for a person the Lord speaks that the sickness is there because of a curse, break the curse and cast out/off the spirit of infirmity, sickness, and or disease. You may do this by saying, In the name of Jesus, I break this curse and I command the spirit of infirmity, sickness and disease to come out or leave. You may at this point encounter some manifestations of the demon coming out but stay in authority over the situation. Some manifestations may include, coughing, yawning, crying, or screaming. Sometimes the demon goes quietly so be very sensitive to the Spirit of the Lord so that He may stay in control of the prayer. If the manifestation of the demon is trying to distract you from continuing the ministry have one of your team members continue the deliverance while the team leader continues to pray for the others who have come for healing. Be aware that demons like to bring attention to themselves and distract from the greater purpose of what the Lord desires to do.

How God anointed and consecrated Jesus of Nazareth with the Holy Spirit and with strength and .ability and power, how He went about doing good and, in particular, curing all who were harassed and oppressed by the power of the devil, for God was with Him.(Acts 10:38) amplified

Reflections

1. Give two scriptural examples when Jesus dealt with evil spirits when healing those who came to Him.

2. Is there a medical solution for the spirit of infirmity?

3. Give two examples where curses are found in scriptures?

4. Give two scriptural examples of demons drawing attention to themselves in the ministry of Jesus or His apostles.

5. Give at least one verse that gives us
the power to break curses?

Notes

HEALING THROUGH GOD'S PRESENCE

There are several ways in which the Lord can bring healing to those with sickness in their bodies without someone laying hands or calling out particular aliments. Though verifiable operations of the healing flow, many do not understand that healing is also contained in the Presence of God. When we enter an atmosphere of true worship at home, in our car or anywhere else for that matter, because the Lord is omnipresent, we can expect Him to heal us because worship ushers in a healing presence.

And it came to pass on a certain day, as He was teaching, that there were Pharisees and doctors of the law sitting by, which were come out of every town of Galilee, and Judaea, and Jerusalem: and the power of the Lord was Present to heal them. (Luke 5:17 KJV)

Here we see the power of the Lord manifested as Jesus was teaching. Anointed teaching or preaching will usher people into the supernatural.

And besought Him that they might only touch the hem of His garment: and as many as touched were made perfectly whole. (Matt. 14:36)

In the presence of God there's fullness of everything you need including healing. Another example is found in the definition of the word healed found in Acts the eighth chapter and the seventh verse:

For unclean spirits, crying with loud voice came out of many that were possessed with them: and many taken with palsies, and that were lame, were healed.

The word healed in this verse is strong's reference #2323 and it means to adore God; to relieve of disease; cure, heal, worship.

In the book of Matthew this definition is used for the word healed all but twice. So, we see that when we adore God and worship Him, His healing presence is ushered in. Worship is a healing presence.

Personally, I like to pray for the sick in an atmosphere of worship because the Lord's voice becomes so clear. Many times, words of knowledge for healing and prophetic words come during times of worship. When we worship Him He not only releases His power to heal, but He will tell you at times exactly what conditions that He is healing. We have a glorious Master. I love the presence of God. There is nothing like it. There is no sacrifice too large, no price too high to pay that can compare to His awesome presence. When we worship the Lord all the heavenly host stands with us. Worshipping the Lord brings us into divine alignment with the Kingdom of Heaven. We know that in God's kingdom there is no sickness or any lack. Worship causes us to be strategically positioned in the Lord. We take our rightful place in Him. God desires us to be a people of His presence. A people who worship know their God and they shall do exploits.

And such as do wickedly against the covenant shall he corrupt by flatteries: but the people that do know their God shall be strong and do exploits. (Dan. 11:32)

You will show me the path of life. In Your presence is fullness of joy, at Your right hand there are pleasures forevermore. (Ps. 16:11)

So that from his body were brought unto the sick handkerchiefs or aprons, and the diseases departed from them, and the evil spirits went out of them. (Acts 19:12)

1. What are some of the benefits of being in the Presence of the Lord?

2. What are some of the benefits of the Presence of the Lord being on you?

3. Does worship aid in healing the sick?

4. What are ways that we can get into an "atmosphere" of healing?

5. Are there other places in scriptures that you can find to support healing in and from the Presence of the Lord?

Notes

HEALING THROURH LAYING ON OF HANDS

And these signs shall follow them that believe; In my name shall they cast out devils; they shall speak with new tongues; They shall take up serpents; and if they drink any deadly thing, it shall not hurt them; they shall lay hands on the sick, and they shall recover. (Mar 16:17-18)

Of the doctrine of baptisms, and of laying on of hands, and of resurrection of the dead, and of eternal judgment. (Heb. 6:2)

According to Hebrews the sixth chapter and the second verse the doctrine of laying on of hands is a principle doctrine of Christ. In other words it is foundational. Though it is a foundational doctrine of Jesus Christ we find that many today do not practice this principle in their everyday lives. The word principle found in Hebrews 6:2 is interpreted as elementary in the amplified version of scripture. *Elementary* means basic, uncomplicated or simple. Many have tried to go on to maturity without the basics and live frustrated Christian lives because of a lack of fruit or evidence of the power of God working on their behalf.

Because of a zeal without proper knowledge to know more about the things of God, many "swallow a camel and strain at a gnat." They go after the deep things of God and nearly drown because they forgot the basics are the things that keep them afloat. Laying on of hands is one of the principle ways that the Lord releases His power.

Now unto Him that is able to do exceeding abundantly above all that we ask or think, according to the power that worketh in us.
(Eph. 3:20)

Through the Holy Spirit that dwells in every believer, God can and is more than willing to release exceeding abundant power according to the measure of the stature of Christ. By the measure of Christ I mean the grace that God has given to every born again believer according to their Kingdom assignment. God desires to release this power through his people because we can't do our part in expanding His Kingdom without it. We have the healing power of

God resident on the inside of us and it needs to be released. Laying hands on the sick is one of the primary signs that Jesus said would follow the believer. As we lay hands on the sick by faith the Lord's healing power will be released without question. But it must be by faith. You can count on it.

There are healing ministers that primarily operate in word of knowledge, some laying on of hands, some by ushering in the presence of the Lord and some a combination of all these and other ways. Did you notice that the word gifts mentioned in I Corinthians chapter 12 is plural? It is plural because there are different administrations or operations of the gift of healing.

REFLECTIONS

1. What is one of the primary ways that
God has ordained that we deliver
healing to the sick?

2. Where does the power come from for
us to lay hands on the sick to see them
recover?

3. Is laying on of hands a principle
doctrine of Christ?

4. Is healing of the sick a way that we
can help to expand the Kingdom of God?
Explain.

5. Give a scriptural example where Jesus laid hands on the sick and they recovered.

Notes

HEALING THROUGH WORD OF KNOWLEDGE

He sent his word, and healed them, and delivered them from their destructions. (Ps.107:20)

For to one is given by the Spirit the word of wisdom; to another the word of knowledge by the same Spirit; (I Cor. 12:8)

Speaking healing through the word of knowledge is a very good way to get the faith level to arise in those who come for ministry. When one hears their particular ailment called out there is a faith that is released in them by that word of knowledge that God has special intentions of healing that problem. One reason is the fact that faith comes by hearing. Although as we have already discussed that there are other ways that the Lord releases His healing virtue, some are more apt to receive through word of knowledge than others. People receive from the Lord in different ways. In the area that I might be more sensitive to the Lord's promptings might not be the way the next person is sensitive to the Lord.

The mature minister will be open to let the Lord have His way.
Now let's go over some of the ways that the word of knowledge operates.

You can <u>HEAR</u> a word of knowledge:

When you're operating in the word of knowledge you will sometimes actually hear the Lord say the area of the body where the healing needs to take place. At times you will even hear the actual condition the person is having problems with.

Joh 4:16-19
  Jesus saith unto her, Go, call thy husband, and come hither.
The woman answered and said, I have no husband. Jesus said unto her, Thou hast well said, I have no husband:
For thou hast had five husbands; and he whom thou now hast is not thy husband: in that saidst thou truly.
The woman saith unto him, Sir, I perceive that thou art a prophet.

You can <u>SEE</u> a word of knowledge:

Nathanael saith unto him, Whence knowest thou me? Jesus answered and

The Lord will show you in a mental
picture of the actual body part that
needs healing in a person. There are also
times when you'll see the specific name
of the ailment.

You can <u>SENSE</u> a word of knowledge:

Words of knowledge and the healing
ministry as a whole have a way of getting
you in touch with the feelings of others
infirmities. At times you will be able to
feel the pain of someone else that the
Lord desires to heal. You may get a
sudden pain in your leg, arm, stomach
or foot that you know are not yours.
These the Lord may have given so that
you may call them out so the person's
faith can be strengthened to be healed.
Also, the knowledge that someone needs
to be healed could come through a
burning sensation in the minister's
hand. Be open to the Spirit of God so
that He may use you the way He desires.

our infirmities; but was in all points tempted like as we are, yet without sin. (Heb 4:15)

You can <u>DREAM</u> a word of knowledge:

You may see in a dream a particular body part that the Lord desires to heal in a service, grocery store or in your own home. Allow the Holy Spirit to have every function of your being at His command. And always remember that the Lord does things decently and in order. You may also ask Him for confirmations. The word of God says that "for a dream comes from a multitude of business."(Eccl. 5:3a) Until you are more familiar with the different administrations of healing ask for confirmations. Confirmations may come through a sense of God's anointing of what you are about to say. It may be the peace of God that you feel about the word of knowledge that confirms the word or it maybe just a knowing, in any event when the time is right move out on it.

If you are in a service you are to use proper protocol of that local assembly when desiring to give a word of knowledge or any form of prophecy.

REFLECTIONS

1. Name three ways to receive a word of knowledge.

2. Give three examples in scripture where word of knowledge is used.

3. What effect does a word of knowledge have on the hearer?

4. Can a word of knowledge be used for more than healing?

5. Is the word of knowledge a gift of the Spirit given by the Lord? Where can it be found?

Notes

Faith for Healing and Miracles

But without faith it is impossible to please him: for he that cometh to God must believe that he is, and that he is a rewarder of them that diligently seek him. (Heb 11:6)

Since through faith we have the substance of things we hope for then we can call those things that be not as if they were and they shall be.
Faith is speaking and believing God with corresponding actions because we know His word is true and His word can not fail. When we do this God promises that we shall have what we say.
Indeed everything we do in Gods Kingdom should be done by faith. If we are not operating in faith the word clearly says we cannot please God. So we can't assume that our prayers will be answered unless accompanied by faith.

Meditating and confessing Gods word brings faith. The more we study and speak His word the more it gets into our heart and becomes our new reality despite outward circumstances. Faith toward God is one of the principles of the doctrines of Christ mentioned in Hebrews chapter 6. So faith is foundational in our walk with the Lord. Psalms eleven verse 3 states,

If the foundations be destroyed what will the righteous do?
And faith is what's needed when contending for healing and miracles. Some healings are miracles, though a miracle is not always a Healing.

To another faith by the same Spirit; to another the Gifts of Healing by the same Spirit; To another the Working of MIRACLES; to another Prophecy; to another Discerning of spirits; to another divers kinds of tongues; to another the interpretation of tongues: (1Co 12:9-10)

And God hath set some in the church, first apostles, secondarily prophets, thirdly teachers, after that MIRACLES, then Gifts of Healings, helps, governments, diversities of tongues. (1Co 12:28)

And God wrought special MIRACLES by the hands of Paul: So that from his body were brought unto the sick handkerchiefs or aprons, and the diseases departed from them, and the evil spirits went out of them. (Act 19:11-12)

Here is the translation for the word miracle in these verses in the Strong's Concordance:

Miracles- ref# 1411-dunamis- *force* (literally or figuratively); specifically miraculous *power* (usually by implication a *miracle* itself): - ability, abundance, meaning, might (-ily, -y, -y deed), (worker of) miracle (-s), power, strength, violence, mighty (wonderful) work.

Dunamis is where we get our word dynamite from. God has set in His Church His Miracle working Power. Everyone does not have the Gifts of Healing or Working of Miracles but all by the Holy Spirit can operate in it to one degree or another.

The gift of working of miracles is so needed in the Body of Christ today. Not only do we need miracles in our physical bodies, but also miracles in our finances, relationships and other areas of life from time to time.
If we don't begin to believe and operate in the gifts of healing and the working of miracles and teach others to do so, the Body of Christ will not be made whole as it should be. I believe that the Lord is

declaring war against sickness, disease, poverty, and all brokenness in the Church today.

Gen 2:7 And the LORD God formed man of the dust of the ground, and breathed into his nostrils the breath of life; and man became a living soul.

This verse is representative of the creative miracle aspect of God. When God formed man from the dust of the ground He created in Him every organ and cell his body would need. Even so today if we have need of replacement parts in our body the Lord has a "warehouse" full of spare parts. The Lord can make us whole again even if He has to replace or recreate the part that's missing. Believe God for every miracle that you need. There's nothing to hard for God, "for all things are possible to them that believe. It takes faith to see the miracle working power of God.

So Abraham prayed unto God: and God healed Abimelech, and his wife, and his maidservants; and they bare children. For the LORD had fast closed up all the

*wombs of the house of Abimelech,
because of Sarah Abraham's wife.
(Gen 20:17-18)*

Healed –ref# 7495- rapha, A primitive
root; properly to *mend* (by stitching),
that is, (figuratively) to *cure*: - cure,
(cause to) heal, physician, repair, X
thoroughly, make whole. (Cure- Restore
to health)

Joh 4:48 Then said Jesus unto him,
Except ye see signs and wonders, ye will
not believe.

Exo 7:9 When Pharaoh shall speak unto
you, saying, Shew a miracle for you:
then thou shalt say unto Aaron, Take thy
rod, and cast *it* before Pharaoh, *and* it
shall become a serpent.

Miracle- ref# 4159- **mo-faith**, From
H3302 in the sense of *conspicuousness*;
a *miracle*; by implication a *token* or
omen: - miracle, sign, wonder (-ed at).

The pronunciation of this Hebrew word
for miracle is very interesting and
truthful. Sometimes it takes a little
mo(re) faith to believe God for a miracle.

Sometimes people won't believe except
they see miracles.

45

Reflections

1. Why can we expect God to show up in our services with healings and miracles?

2. Does everyone have the Gifts of Healing? Or Working of Miracles?

3. Can God create new body parts in us? Give a scripture to support your answer.

4. What key ingredient helps us to work miracles?

5. Why is it important to have faith for healing and miracles when ministering to the lost?

Notes

OUR RESPONSIBILITIES

BE HONEST WITH YOURSELF

When dealing with lingering health issues one must begin to examine himself also to see where the problem lies. We are not saying become guilt conscience or put yourself under condemnation, but sometimes the blockage lies within. There are factors such as stress, worry, unforgiveness, bitterness, pride and envy that will contribute to unanswered prayers. These attitudes are out of line with the mind of Christ and can cause malfunctions in our faith and bodies.

Let's look at unforgiveness for a moment. In Matthew the eighteenth chapter we see a situation where someone did not forgive a debt as even as they were forgiven of their debts. We pick up the story at verse thirty-three:

Shouldest not thou also have had compassion on thy fellow servant, even as I had pity on thee? And his lord was wroth, and delivered him to the tormentors, till he should pay all that was due unto him. So likewise shall my

*heavenly Father do also unto you, if ye
from your hearts forgive not every one
his brother their trespasses.
  (Matt. 18:33-35)*

The word tormentors here is strong's
ref. # 930 (*basanistes*) and it means a
torturer. It is from ref# 928 (*basanizo*)
which means to torture:- pain, toil,
torment, toss, vex.

So we see here that unforgiveness opens
the door to one being tormented. It is
not the Lord's will that this should
happen but we take things into our own
hands when we will not submit to His
perfect will.

Also tormented (Basanizo) is the word
used in Matthew 8:6 and is clearly tied
to sickness:

*And saying, Lord, my servant lieth at
home sick of the palsy, grievously
tormented.*

 And again It is also tied to ref# 931
(*basanos*) which is the word used in
Matthew 4:24 and is also linked with
sickness and diseases.

And his fame went throughout all Syria: and they brought unto him all sick people that were taken with <u>divers diseases and torments</u>, and those which were possessed with devils, and those which were lunatick, and those that had the palsy; and he healed them. (Matt 4:24)

So we see here how unforgiveness can be tied to sickness and disease. So it is our responsibility to make sure that we forgive others as Christ has forgiven us. Now I do not believe that the Lord will put sickness or disease on anyone but I do believe that we can walk from under the Lord's covering through disobedience and other forms of sins that will cause us to be vulnerable to disease.

I, on a more personal note, several years ago, was holding unforgiveness in my heart toward this particular individual. At the same time I had started to develop an arthritic condition in my shoulders. That seems to have come from nowhere. And one day I was listening to this well known Christian TV host who is very strong in word of knowledge healing. He began to speak about how holding unforgiveness can cause arthritis. And immediately I began to search my heart to see if I had fallen into unforgiveness toward anyone. After the Lord brought a person to mind I forgave them from my heart and was healed! We do have a responsibility in our own healing.

Discerning the Lord's body is another way we can defeat sickness and diseases.

And when He had given thanks, He brake it, and said, Take, eat: this is My body, which is broken for you: this do in remembrance of Me. After the same manner also He took the cup, when He had supped, saying, This cup is the new testament in My blood: this do ye, as oft as ye drink it, in remembrance of Me. For as often as ye eat this bread, and drink this cup, ye don show the Lord's death till He come. Wherefore whosoever shall eat this bread, and drink this cup of the Lord, unworthily, shall be guilty of the body and blood of the Lord. But let a man examine himself, and so let him eat of that bread. And drink of that cup. For he that eats and drinks unworthily, eats and drinks damnation to himself, not discerning the Lord's body <u>for this cause many are weak and sickly among you, and many sleep</u>. For if we would judge ourselves,

The word weak in verse 31 is strong's ref#770 (*astheneo*) to be feeble, be diseased, impotent, be sick, be made weak.

Our attitude towards our brothers and sisters in Christ has a lot to do with our sickness and/or healing. We must learn to love others as Christ loved us, there's no way around it. Jesus gave us such a perfect example to follow by His death and resurrection.

We must become so intimate with the Father that His heart becomes our heart. The Father wants so much to reconcile us unto Himself that He is willing to forgive us of some of the most hideous transgressions if we only turn away from them and accept what Christ has done for us on the cross.

So also we must have this ministry of reconciliation that we may cause men to be reconnected to their heavenly Father by laying down our lives and our rights for the sake of the guilty and pardoning them of their transgressions against us.

We must heed the word of the Lord
through Apostle Paul and not be a
partaker of the body and blood of Christ
unworthily.

1. Name three Factors that can contribute to unanswered Prayer?

2. Why is it so important to forgive others?

3. What is one of the results of not Discerning the Lord's Body?

4. According to Matthew 18: 33 what is a key ingredient for forgiveness?

5. In your own words, what should we do if we have a problem with forgiveness? Can you name a scripture?

Notes

POWER OF THE KINGDOM: RECEIVING AND RELEASING

WARNING: It is dangerous to desire the gifts and the Power of God without an intimate relationship with the Father.

Many will say to me in that day, Lord, Lord, have we not prophesied in thy name? and in thy name have cast out devils? and in thy name done many wonderful works?
And then will I profess unto them, I never knew you: depart from me, ye that work iniquity. (Matt. 7:22-23)

FIRST THINGS FIRST

Master, which is the great commandment in the law? Jesus said unto him, Thou shalt love the Lord thy God with all thy heart, and with all thy soul, and with all thy mind.
This is the first and great commandment. And the second is like unto it, Thou shalt love thy neighbour as thyself. On these two commandments hang all the law and the prophets. (Mat 22:36-40)

Jesus is asked here, which is the first commandment. If God is not first our good works will become dead ritualism and will lead astray our hearts. In some cases it will make us prideful and self-righteous. We should be moved by the heart and will of God and not by need only. It's the romance of the Gospel. Love Him more than anything.

DOMINION

Christ in you is the hope of the glory to release Gods power in the earth realm. When we walk even as Jesus walked on the earth, in grace and truth, we will begin to see the power manifestations that He saw. Christ knew who He was when He was on earth. He knew He was created in the image and likeness of His Father even as we are (Heb. 1:1-3, Gen. 1:27). He knew His purpose and assignment and He did not let anyone or anything deter Him from it. God's purpose is His Kingdom being established on earth.

Jesus came to show us how to establish Gods Kingdom on earth as it is in Heaven. He gave us perfect examples on how it should primarily be done. Jesus expanded the Kingdom by exercising authority and dominion over demons, religion, sickness, disease, poverty, and lack, etc. We are to take that example and cause the kingdoms of this world to become the Kingdoms of our Lord's and His Christ (Rev. 11:15).

As we exercise dominion in the name of Jesus in our spheres of influence the wisdom and the power of the Kingdom will be released to assist us. Remember God gave dominion of the earth to man. So, God needs man to release Him to act on earth. This is done primarily through our prayers, prophecies and decrees. Without the Lord we can do nothing (John 15:5). Without God we cannot, without man God will not. We are not waiting on God; God is waiting on us to move in our Kingdom assignment so He can legally assist us and release His power.

So, as we pray, decree, prophesy, do prophetic acts, etc. let's do all with a Kingdom mentality. For as we seek first His Kingdom and His righteousness all these other things shall be added unto us.

And such as do wickedly against the covenant shall he corrupt by flatteries: but the people that do know their God shall be strong, and do exploits. (Daniel 11:32)

PRAYER AND FASTING

Confess to one another therefore your faults (your slips, your false steps, your offenses, your sins) and pray also for one another, that you may be healed and restored to a spiritual tone of mind and heart. The earnest (heartfelt, continued) prayer of a righteous man makes tremendous power available dynamic in its working. (James 5:16 amp.)

The type of prayer that releases the power of God is earnest and heartfelt. Some synonyms for earnest are serious, deep and intense. We must be focused and sincere when we pray believing in faith that God will honor His word.

Some synonyms for tremendous are: great and incredible. Your Kingdom focused prayers will release great and incredible or hard to believe miracles. For, He is able to do exceedingly and abundantly above all that you can ask or even think (Eph. 3:20)!

It is after an all night prayer that Jesus is propelled in a tremendous healing and deliverance anointing (Lk. 6:12-19), where He healed all that came unto him. Effective fervent prayer releases the anointing of Power!

We will dedicate more time on prayer in
a later chapter.

Likewise fasting also releases
tremendous power to lift heavy burdens,
to destroy yokes and cause healing to
come forth speedily (Is. 58:6, 8).
Fasting subdues the flesh and allows the
Spirit to take control. That which is born
of flesh is flesh, and that which is born
of Spirit is Spirit (John 3:6). The Lord
can release unlimited power through a
yielded vessel. Fasting is a tool we can
use to get us to a point of tremendous
release of Gods power. Fasting helps us
to be humble and chaste before the Lord
(Ps. 35:13, 69:10). To be humble means
to be meek or lowly. Jesus desires us to
be this way because it causes us to rest
in Him (Matt. 11:29).

Reflections

1. Why can it be dangerous to operate in the gifts of the Spirit without an intimate relationship with the Father?

2. What are the two greatest commandments based on?

3. Are there any conditions to be endued with the Power of God?

4. Does prayer and fasting play a role in releasing the power of God? How so?

5. Is holiness important when walking in the Power of God?

Notes

PURPOSE OF POWER

TO EXPRESS COMPASSION

The Spirit of the Lord is upon me, because he hath anointed me to preach the gospel to the poor; he hath sent me to heal the brokenhearted, to preach deliverance to the captives, and recovering of sight to the blind, to set at liberty them that are bruised, To preach the acceptable year of the Lord. (Luk 4:18-19)

In our continuing the ministry of Jesus in serving man kind for the purposes of reconciliation, we must remember that it was His compassion that motivated the release of healing into the lives of those He ministered to (Matt. 9:36, 14:14, 18:27, Mk. 1:41). And of course His passion of the cross made it all available for us (Acts 1:3, Is. 53:4-5).

TO GATHER THE HARVEST

And Jesus went about all the cities and villages, teaching in their synagogues, and preaching the gospel of the kingdom, and healing every sickness and every disease among the people. But when he saw the multitudes, he was

*moved with compassion on them,
because they fainted, and were
scattered abroad, as sheep having no
shepherd. Then saith he unto his
disciples, The harvest truly is plenteous,
but the labourers are few;
Pray ye therefore the Lord of the
harvest, that he will send forth
labourers into his harvest.*
 (Matthew 9:35-38)
*And when he had called unto him his
twelve disciples, he gave them power
against unclean spirits, to cast them
out, and to heal all manner of sickness
and all manner of disease.
And as ye go, preach, saying, The
kingdom of heaven is at hand.*

*Heal the sick, cleanse the lepers, raise
the dead, cast out devils: freely ye have
received, freely give.*
 (Matthew 10:1, 7-8)

Healing, miracles and deliverance are
harvesting tools to reap the harvest of
the nations.

REGIONAL TRANSFORMATION

*Therefore they that were scattered
abroad went every where preaching the
word. Then Philip went down to the city
of Samaria, and preached Christ unto*

*them. And the people with one accord
gave heed unto those things which
Philip spake, hearing and seeing the
miracles which he did. For unclean
spirits, crying with loud voice, came out
of many that were possessed with
them: and many taken with palsies,
and that were lame, were healed. And
there was great joy in that city.*
(Acts 8:4-8)

The power of God released through
compassionate vessels will not only
bring transformation to individuals but
can impact, with strategic planning an
entire city or region, because His
Kingdom rules over all (Ps. 103:19).

Reflections

1. What is one of the purposes of God displaying His power?

2. In what ways does God display His power?

3. How is the power of God used as a tool to gather the harvest of souls?

4. Can we buy the power of God or is it freely given?

5. What kingdom has power over all other kingdoms including sickness and disease?

Notes

THE POWER OF PRAYER

Confess to one another therefore your faults (your slips, your false steps, your offenses, your sins) and pray also for one another, that you may be healed and restored to a spiritual tone of mind and heart. The earnest (heartfelt, continued) prayer of a righteous man makes tremendous power available dynamic in its working.
(James 5:16 amp.)

First of all we see to have effective prayer one must have a clear mind and heart. If there is something affecting our love walk it can and will hinder our prayers. The spirit of offense and sin keeps us from praying with fervency and conviction. If we want to see effective prayers we must have a repentant attitude in our relationships and the circumstances of life. The Lord is more than willing to help us to do this. I believe that many of our prayers go unanswered because of the condition of the heart of the one that is praying.

And when you stand praying, forgive, if you have ought against any: that your Father also which is in heaven may forgive you your trespasses. (Mark 11:25)

The Lord cares very much about our attitude when we pray. Many prayers that are not prayed out of a repentant and forgiving heart are often soulish (carnal) and selfish and that's not the will of God.

That is because the mind of the flesh with its carnal thoughts and purposes is hostile to God, for it does not submit itself to God's Law; indeed it cannot. (Romans 8:7 amp.)

When we pray according to God's word we are releasing the divine will and council of the Lord, for the Holy Spirit is making intercessions through us.

Likewise the Spirit also helpeth our infirmities: for we know not what we should pray for as we ought: but the Spirit itself maketh intercession for us with groanings which cannot be uttered. (Romans 8:26)

So if we want to walk in the power that
is available to us through prayer we
must be quick to repent and slow to
wrath.

*Wherefore, my beloved brethren, let
every man be swift to hear, slow to
speak, slow to wrath:
For the wrath of man worketh not the
righteousness of God. (James 1:19-20)*

It is when our prayers are from a
righteous (in right standing with God),
earnest (zealous and sincere) heart and
is persistent that we see tremendous
power released on our behalf.

This part of James 5:16 is explained in
the seventeenth and eighteenth verse of
James by the prayer of Elijah.

*Elijah was a human being with a
nature such as we have (with feelings,
affections, and a constitution like ours);
and he prayed earnestly for it not to
rain, and no rain fell on the earth for
three years and six months. And then
he prayed again and the heavens
supplied rain and land produced its
crops as usual. (James 5:17-18 amp.)*

Elijahs prayer was continual until God gave him a sign (a small cloud) or a point of release. He had to birth it through. The Lord loves it when His children show faith enough to birth through their miracle.

As Daniel saw, a lot of times the prayers are answered right away, but we have an enemy that can hinder the manifestation of it. But thanks be unto God who always gives us the victory. He will see us through if we faint not.

Then said he unto me, Fear not, Daniel: for from the first day that thou didst set thine heart to understand, and to chasten thyself before thy God, thy words were heard, and I am come for thy words. But the prince of the kingdom of Persia withstood me one and twenty days: but, lo, Michael, one of the chief princes, came to help me; and I remained there with the kings of Persia. Now I am come to make thee understand what shall befall thy people in the latter days: for yet the vision is for many days. (Dan 10:12-14)

*And let us not be weary in well doing:
for in due season we shall reap, if we
faint not. (Gal. 6:9)*

Whenever you see genuine miracles of
God being worked through an individual
rest assured that someone paid a price
in sincere heartfelt fervent prayer
behind the scenes.

Reflections

1. What kind of prayer makes tremendous power available?

2. Are there any criteria to enter into effectual prayer?

3. Can we pray sincerely with a carnal mindset? Can a carnal mind subject itself to the Spirit of God?

4. Should we pray about a particular thing until we get tired of it or until God gives us a sign such as peace?

5. Is there a price to pay to see miracles manifested in your life or ministry? If so what is it?

Notes

SCRIPTUAL REASONS WHY PEOPLE GET HEALED

He sent <u>His Word</u>, and healed them, and delivered them from their destructions. (Psa 107:20)

*But He was wounded for our transgressions, He was bruised for our iniquities: the chastisement of our peace was upon Him; and with <u>His stripes</u> we are healed.
(Isa 53:5)*

And Jesus went forth, and saw a great multitude, and was <u>moved with compassion</u> toward them, and he healed their sick. (Mat 14:14)

*For He had healed many; insomuch that they <u>pressed</u> upon Him for to touch Him, as many as had plagues.
(Mar 3:10)*

And Jesus went about all Galilee, <u>Teaching</u> in their synagogues, and <u>Preaching the gospel of the kingdom</u>, and healing all manner of sickness and

all manner of disease among the people.
(Mat 4:23)

And they went out, and preached that
men should Repent. And they cast out
many devils, and anointed with oil
many that were sick, and healed them.
(Mar 6:12-13)

And as He was yet a coming, the devil
threw him down, and tare him. And
Jesus rebuked the unclean spirit, and
healed the child, and delivered him
again to his father.
(Luk 9:42)

But Jesus turned him about, and when
he saw her, he said, Daughter, be of
good comfort; _thy Faith hath made thee
whole_. And the woman was made
whole from that hour.
(Mat 9:22)

And he spake a parable unto them to
this end, that men ought _always to
pray, and not to faint;_ (Luk 18:1)

Notes

SCRIPTUAL REASONS WHY PEOPLE DON'T GET HEALED

Son of man, prophesy against the shepherds of Israel, prophesy, and say unto them, Thus saith the Lord GOD unto the shepherds; Woe be to the shepherds of Israel that do feed themselves! <u>should not the shepherds feed the flocks</u>? The <u>diseased have ye not strengthened</u>, <u>neither have ye healed that which was sick</u>, neither have ye bound up that which was broken, neither have ye brought again that which was driven away, neither have ye sought that which was lost; but with force and with cruelty have ye ruled them. (Eze 34:2, 4)

And he could there do no mighty work, save that he laid his hands upon a few sick folk, and healed them. And he marvelled because of their <u>Unbelief</u>. And he went round about the villages, teaching. (Mar 6:5-6)

And Jesus said unto them, <u>Because of your unbelief</u>: for verily I say unto you, If ye have faith as a grain of mustard seed, ye shall say unto this mountain, Remove hence to yonder place; and it *shall remove; and nothing shall be impossible unto you. (Mat 17:20)*

<u>Confess your faults</u> one to another, and <u>pray one for another</u>, that ye may be healed. The effectual fervent prayer of a righteous man availeth much. (Jas 5:16)

And he said, I will hide my face from them, I will see what their end shall be: for they are a very <u>froward generation, children in whom is no faith</u>. (Deu 32:20)

And immediately Jesus stretched forth his hand, and caught him, and said unto him, O thou of <u>little faith</u>, wherefore didst thou <u>doubt</u>? (Mat 14:31)

Then Jesus answered and said, O <u>faithless and perverse</u> generation, how long shall I be with you? how long shall I suffer you? bring him hither to me.

And <u>Jesus rebuked the devil</u>; and he departed out of him: and the child was cured from that very hour.
(Mat 17:17-18)

Notes

Notes

Notes

Notes